Retargeting Mastery: Winning Sales with Online Strategies

B. Vincent

Published by RWG Publishing, 2023.

RETARGETING MASTERY: WINNING SALES WITH ONLINE STRATEGIES

First edition. April 6, 2023.

Written by B. Vincent.

Also by B. Vincent

Affiliate Marketing
Affiliate Marketing
Affiliate Marketing

Standalone
Business Employee Discipline
Affiliate Recruiting
Business Layoffs & Firings
Business and Entrepreneur Guide
Business Remote Workforce
Career Transition
Project Management
Precision Targeting
Professional Development
Strategic Planning
Content Marketing
Imminent List Building
Getting Past GateKeepers
Banner Ads
Bookkeeping
Bridge Pages
Business Acquisition

Business Bogging
Business Communication Course
Marketing Automation
Better Meetings
Business Conflict Resolution
Business Culture Course
Conversion Optimization
Creative Solutions
Employee Recruitment
Startup Capital
Employee Incentives
Employee Mentoring
Followership
Servant Leadership
Human Resources
Team Building
Freelancing
Funnel Building
Geo Targeting
Goal Setting
Immanent List Building
Lead Generation
Leadership Course
Leadership Transition
Leadership vs Management
LinkedIn Ads
LinkedIn Marketing
Messenger Marketing
New Management
Newsfeed Ads
Search Ads
Online Learning
Sales Webinars

Table of Contents

Chapter 1: Understanding Retargeting: The Basics and Beyond

———

When it comes to marketing strategies, retargeting is one of the most important ones for companies that want to boost their online sales. Targeting people who have interacted with your website or brand in the past and displaying ads that are specific to them in order to entice them to come back and make a purchase is what it means to engage in retargeting.

Putting a small piece of code, known as a pixel, on your website is the first step in retargeting, and it's also the most fundamental step. This pixel records information about the actions taken by visitors, such as the web pages they view and the items they add to their shopping cart. Using this information, you will be able to create targeted advertisements for those visitors that will appear to them when they are using search engines, social media platforms, or other websites.

However, retargeting is not limited to simply following visitors around the web and displaying advertisements to them. Using data to create personalized experiences that are tailored to the requirements of individual customers and boost sales is the goal. In order to accomplish this, businesses need to go beyond the fundamentals and gain an understanding of the various types of retargeting strategies as well as how each of these strategies can be used to engage customers.

The use of dynamic retargeting is an example of an effective retargeting strategy. This strategy entails the creation of advertisements that showcase the specific products that website visitors viewed on your site or added to their shopping carts. Customers will always see the most recent information about your products when you use dynamic retargeting because it utilizes product feeds to keep the advertisements up to date in real time. This tactic is especially useful for e-commerce businesses, as it has the potential to cut down on the number of customers who abandon their shopping carts and boost overall sales.

Sequential retargeting is an additional important tactic that should not be overlooked. This entails displaying a series of advertisements to customers that are adapted to their actions while visiting your website. You could, for instance, show a visitor an ad for a product that they viewed on your website, followed by an ad that offers a discount code for that product, and finally, an ad that creates a sense of urgency by highlighting the fact that the product is running low on stock. You can develop a relationship with prospective customers and encourage them to make a purchase by using sequential retargeting to send them targeted advertisements in a series.

In addition to these strategies, businesses may also make use of retargeting in order to target particular subsets of the audience they are addressing. You could, for instance, create advertisements that are directed toward customers who have deleted items from their shopping carts or who have returned to your website on multiple occasions but have not yet made a purchase. You can increase the likelihood that individuals from these groups will return to your website and make a purchase by developing ads that are specifically targeted to these groups.

Understanding the fundamentals of retargeting, in general, is essential for any company that wants to increase the amount of money it makes through online sales. But in order to truly master retargeting, you need to go beyond the fundamentals and investigate the various strategies and methods that can assist you in engaging your audience and driving conversions. Only then will you be able to call yourself a master. You will be able to generate personalized experiences for your customers, which will both satisfy their requirements and drive sales for your company.

Chapter 2: Building a Strong Foundation: Setting Up Your Retargeting Campaign

When it comes to conducting retargeting campaigns that are successful, laying a solid foundation is absolutely necessary. It is possible that your campaigns will not produce the results you are looking for if they are not properly planned and organized. In the following chapter, we will go over the primary actions that must be taken in order to construct a solid basis for your retargeting campaign.

The first step is to determine your objectives.

Establishing your objectives is the first thing you need to do in order to construct a solid base for your retargeting initiative. What are some of the goals that you hope to accomplish with this campaign? Do you want to raise the amount of people visiting your website, bring in new leads, or push more sales? You will be able to determine the best retargeting strategies to achieve your goals if you first identify those goals.

Install the Retargeting Pixel as the Second Step

After you have decided what you want to accomplish, the next step is to put a retargeting pixel on your website so that you can track visitors after they leave. This pixel, which is a very small piece of code, monitors the actions taken by people who visit your website. Installing the pixel allows you to collect useful data on the actions of visitors, which can then be used to generate more specific advertisements.

Step 3: Define Your Target Audience

Your ability to define your target audience is going to be the determining factor in whether or not your retargeting campaign is successful. Who exactly are you hoping to reach with your advertisements? You will be able to produce advertisements that cater to the specific interests and requirements of your target demographic if you first identify that demographic. You can define your target audience by using data obtained from the retargeting pixel, in addition to data obtained from other sources, such as customer demographics and behavior.

Step 4: Construct the Creative for Your Ad

The next thing you need to do is work on the creative for your advertisement. Your advertisements need to be appealing to the eye, interesting to read, and pertinent to the people you are trying to reach. You can create effective ad creative by making use of a variety of strategies, such as dynamic product ads, personalized messaging, and visually captivating content that grabs the audience's attention.

Step 5: Set Your Budget and Bidding Strategy

Before you get started with your retargeting campaign, you need to figure out your spending limit and your approach to bidding. What is the maximum amount that you are willing to spend on your campaign, and what is the maximum amount that you are willing to bid for each ad impression? Your budget and strategy for placing bids will differ according to your objectives, audience demographics, and the level of competition in your sector.

Launching and Keeping an Eye on Your Campaign is the Sixth Step.

You will be able to start your retargeting campaign as soon as you have finished the steps that came before it. It is important to monitor the performance of your campaign as it is running so that any necessary adjustments can be made. You can evaluate the efficiency of your campaign by using metrics like click-through rates, conversion rates, and return on ad spend, and then make adjustments to improve the campaign's overall performance based on your findings.

You will be able to lay a solid groundwork for your retargeting campaign if you follow these steps to the letter. You will be able to develop successful marketing campaigns for your company if you have a comprehensive understanding of your objectives, intended audience, ad creative, budget, and bidding strategy. These elements will allow you to generate results that will drive sales.

Chapter 3: Targeting the Right Audience: Identifying Your Ideal Customer

Targeting the appropriate audience is one of the aspects of retargeting that is considered to be among the most important. It is unlikely that your retargeting campaign will be as successful as you would like if you do not have a crystal clear understanding of your ideal customer. In this chapter, we will discuss the key steps involved in identifying your ideal customer and targeting them with your retargeting campaign. Your ideal customer is the person who has the most money to spend on your product or service.

First, you will need to define your ideal customer.

Developing a customer persona should be the first thing you do when trying to determine who your ideal client is. This persona represents your ideal customer and includes demographic information such as age, gender, location, and income as well as psychographic information such as interests, values, and behaviors. In addition, this persona includes information about the customer's demographics. The development of a customer persona enables the production of advertisements that are specifically geared toward the customers' particular preferences and requirements.

Step 2: Determine Who Your Ideal Customers Are by Analyzing the Data

Following the creation of your customer persona, the next step is to identify your target audience by making use of the data at your disposal. In order to collect information about your audience, you can make use of a wide variety of data sources, such as website analytics, customer surveys, and the insights provided by social media. The characteristics of your target audience, such as their browsing behavior, purchase history, and interests, can be determined with the help of the data presented here.

Step 3: Segment Your Audience

After you have determined who your target demographic is, the next step is to categorize each member of that demographic. When you segment your audience, you divide them up into different groups according to the characteristics they share. You could, for instance, divide your audience into segments according to their previous purchases, their browsing habits, or their demographic information. You will be able to create advertisements that cater to the specific requirements and interests of each segment of your audience if you segment your audience first.

Create Custom Audiences is the fourth step.

Creating custom audiences is an efficient additional method you can use to zero in on your ideal customer. Custom audiences are groups of people who have already engaged with your brand in some way, such as by visiting your website, signing up for your newsletter, or making a purchase. These individuals can then be targeted with advertisements that are specific to their interests. Through the use of custom audiences, you are able to generate advertisements that are highly personalized and pertinent to the interests of the target audience.

Step 5: Use Lookalike Audiences

You can target new customers who share similar characteristics with your existing audience by making use of lookalike audiences, in addition to custom audiences, if you want to expand your customer base. Lookalike audiences are created by conducting an analysis of the characteristics of your current audience and locating people who have characteristics that are comparable to those of your existing audience. You can reach new customers who are likely to be interested in your brand if you target audiences that are similar to those you already have.

The sixth step is to continually monitor and adjust your targeting strategy.

After you have established your retargeting campaigns and determined your target audience, it is essential to continually monitor and improve your targeting strategy in order to maximize its effectiveness. You can evaluate the effectiveness of your campaigns and make adjustments as necessary by using metrics such as click-through rates, conversion rates, and return on ad spend. You can make sure that the right people are being reached by your retargeting campaigns and that they are producing results for your company if you continually work to improve the targeting strategy you use.

When it comes to retargeting, one of the most important things you can do is figure out who your ideal customer is. You will be able to design successful campaigns that are successful in reaching the right people and driving results for your company if you define your customer persona, use data to identify your target audience, segment your audience, create custom and lookalike audiences, and continuously refine your targeting strategy.

Chapter 4: Maximizing Your Ad Spend: Budgeting and Bidding Strategies

W hen it comes to retargeting, it is essential to make the most of the money you spend on advertisements. You want to make sure that your advertisements are getting seen by the appropriate audience and producing results for your company. In this chapter, we will go over the key strategies for budgeting and bidding that will allow you to get the most out of your advertising dollars.

Step 1: Determine Your Budget

Establishing a spending limit is the first thing you need to do in order to make the most of your advertising dollars. What kind of budget do you have in mind for the retargeting campaign you want to run? Your budget will be determined by the overall marketing goals you have for your company as well as the size of your company. It is essential to establish a spending plan that is in line with your resources and allows you to communicate with the people you want to reach without going bankrupt.

Step 2. Select Your Preferred Approach to the Bidding Process

The next thing you need to do is choose a strategy for your bid. The process of determining how much you are willing to pay for each advertisement impression is referred to as bidding. You have a number of options available to you when it comes to bidding strategies, such as cost per click (also written as CPC), cost per thousand impressions (also written as CPM), and cost per action (CPA). Because each strategy for placing bids carries both benefits and drawbacks, it is essential to select the one that is best suited to your objectives and financial constraints.

Step 3: Modify Your Offers According to How Well They Perform

After you have started your retargeting campaign, it is essential to make adjustments to your bids based on how well the campaign is doing. If your advertisements are performing well, you should consider raising your bids in order to communicate with a wider audience. If your advertisements are not performing as well as you had hoped, you might want to consider lowering your bids or modifying your approach to targeting.

The next step is to adjust the frequency caps.

Setting frequency caps is another essential strategy that can help you get the most out of your advertising budget. The number of times an individual will be exposed to your advertisement is governed by frequency caps. You can prevent ad fatigue and lower engagement with your audience by limiting how often your advertisements are displayed. This can be accomplished through the use of frequency caps.

Step 5: Use Ad Scheduling

The process of scheduling when your advertisements will appear can be broken down into specific times of the day or days of the week. You can make sure that your ads are displayed at the times of day when your target audience is the most likely to be online by using a tool called ad scheduling. This can help to increase engagement and make the most of the money you spend on advertisements.

Step 6: Track the Results of Your Advertisements

Last but not least, it is essential to keep track of how well your advertisements are performing in order to guarantee that your retargeting campaigns are producing fruitful outcomes for your company. You can evaluate the effectiveness of your campaigns and make adjustments as necessary by using metrics such as click-through rates, conversion rates, and return on ad spend.

When it comes to retargeting, it is essential to make the most of the money you spend on advertisements. You are able to develop successful marketing campaigns for your company by determining your budget, selecting the appropriate bidding strategy, modifying your bids based on performance, establishing frequency caps, making use of ad scheduling, and monitoring the performance of your advertisements. These steps will allow you to connect with the appropriate individuals and generate results for your company.

Chapter 5: Crafting Effective Retargeting Ads: Copywriting and Design Tips

---

It is essential to craft effective retargeting ads if you want to drive results and maximize the effectiveness of your advertising spend. Your advertisements have to be appealing to the eye, interesting to read, and pertinent to the people you are trying to reach. In this section, we will go over some of the most important copywriting and design tips that will assist you in developing effective retargeting ads.

First Piece of Advice: Make Use of Eye-Catching Visuals

Utilizing visuals that are captivating is the first step to taking your retargeting ads from good to great. Your advertisements have to stand out from the rest of the pack and get the attention of the people you are trying to reach. Your advertisements can be made to appear more visually appealing by incorporating a number of different visual elements, such as vibrant colors, high-quality images, and bold typography.

Tip 2: Ensure that Your Messages Are Understandable and Brief

When it comes to the writing of copy for retargeting ads, it is critical to ensure that your messaging is both clear and concise. Your advertisements should convey your message in just a few words or phrases to avoid overwhelming the people you are trying to reach with an excessive amount of information. To encourage clicks and conversions, use headlines that are succinct and attention-grabbing, as well as calls to action.

Use Personalized and Dynamic Creativity, as the Third Piece of Advice

Personalization and dynamic creative are two additional methods that are useful for retargeting advertisements. The process of tailoring your advertisements to the preferences and actions of your target audience is an example of personalization. Utilizing product feeds to create advertisements that feature specific products that your target audience has viewed or added to their cart is an example of what is known as dynamic creative. Creating advertisements that are highly relevant to your target audience and increasing the likelihood of conversion can be accomplished through the utilization of personalization and dynamic creative.

The fourth piece of advice is to emphasize your one-of-a-kind selling proposition (USP)

Your unique selling proposition, also known as USP, is the aspect of your brand that distinguishes it from others in its industry. It is essential to highlight your unique selling proposition (USP) in the ads that you use for retargeting if you want to increase clicks and conversions. Make sure the messaging you use conveys to your target audience why your brand is so special and why they should care about it.

5. Make Use of a Sense of Urgency and Scarcity

Utilizing a sense of urgency and scarcity is another powerful strategy for developing effective retargeting ads. To create a sense of urgency that motivates your target audience to take action, you can use phrases like "limited time offer" or "while supplies last." This can be accomplished through the use of the word "urgency." Scarcity marketing involves drawing attention to the fact that a particular good or service is in limited supply. This can generate a feeling of immediacy and encourage consumers to make purchases.

Tip No. 6: Analyze and Improve the Performance of Your Ads

In conclusion, it is essential to test and improve the performance of your retargeting advertisements in order to guarantee that they are productive for your company. You can run multiple tests with different iterations of your advertisements, such as those with varying images or headlines, to determine which one is most successful. You can also evaluate the efficacy of your advertisements by using metrics such as click-through rates and conversion rates, and you can make adjustments to them as necessary.

In conclusion, creating ads for retargeting that are effective is essential if you want to drive results and make the most of your advertising budget. You can create successful advertising campaigns that engage your target audience and drive results for your business by making use of eye-catching visuals, keeping your messaging clear and concise, using personalization and dynamic creative, highlighting your unique selling proposition (USP), using urgency and scarcity, and testing and optimizing your advertisements.

Chapter 6: A/B Testing: Optimizing Your Ads for Maximum Conversions

———

Testing with the A/B method is an essential strategy for optimizing your retargeting ads to achieve the highest possible conversion rate. You can determine the most effective messaging, imagery, and targeting strategies for your target audience by testing different variations of your ads and seeing which ones perform the best. In this chapter, we will go over the primary steps involved in performing A/B testing on your retargeting ads.

First Step: Determine Your Testing Objectives

The first thing you need to do before running an A/B test on your retargeting ads is to determine what you want to learn from the test. What do you hope to learn through the testing that you are conducting? Do you want to increase the number of people who visit your website, increase the number of people who convert, or improve your click-through rates? You will be able to determine the testing strategies that will yield the best results if you first establish your testing goals.

Step 2. Determine Which Variables You Will Test

The following step is to select the variables that will be tested. These are the aspects of your advertisement that will be subjected to testing, such as the headline, the image, the call to action, or the targeting strategy. It is essential that you select variables that are likely to have a substantial influence on the performance of your advertisement.

Create Your Testing Groups as the Third Step

After you have determined the variables that will be tested, the next step is to establish the groups that will be used for the test. These are the subsets of individuals who will be exposed to the various iterations of your advertisements. You can divide your audience into equal groups, or you can use a percentage split to test a smaller sample size.

Step 4: Put Your Hypotheses to the Test

After you have established your testing groups, the next step is to carry out your tests in their respective environments. Performing this step entails presenting the various iterations of your advertisements to each group and analyzing how well they perform. You can evaluate the effectiveness of each variation by using metrics such as click-through rates, conversion rates, and return on ad spend.

Step 5: Conduct an Evaluation of Your Results

Following the completion of your tests, the following step is to conduct an analysis of the results. Examine the data for repeating structures or trends in order to establish which variations performed the best. You should also consider segmenting your data based on the demographic or behavioral characteristics of your subjects in order to determine which groups responded most favorably to each change.

Implement Your Winning Variation is the Sixth Step.

Implementing the winning variation in your retargeting campaign is the final step to take after you have determined which variation performed the best. Make use of the successful variation in future ads, and continue to test new variations, to ensure that your ads are always optimized for the highest possible number of conversions.

To summarize, A/B testing is an essential method for optimizing your retargeting ads in order to achieve the highest possible conversion rate. You can effectively create campaigns that engage your target audience and drive results for your business if you first determine your testing goals, then select your testing variables, create your testing groups, run your tests, analyze your results, and then implement the winning variation.

Chapter 7: The Power of Video: Incorporating Video Ads into Your Retargeting Campaign

---

Retargeting campaigns can benefit greatly from the utilization of video advertisements. Text and still images on their own are not sufficient to convey feeling or tell a story; however, video has the ability to do all three. In this chapter, we will discuss the advantages of including video advertisements in your retargeting campaign, as well as how to effectively create video advertisements for your campaign.

Advantages of Using Video Ads

Including video advertisements as part of your retargeting campaign can confer a number of benefits to your business. Just a few of them are as follows:

Video advertisements are significantly more engaging to viewers than text or image advertisements are. They are able to evoke feelings and attract attention in a way that other forms of advertising simply cannot.

Higher Conversion Rates Compared to Other Ad Formats Research has shown that video advertisements have higher conversion rates than other types of advertisements. They have the potential to deliver a more engrossing experience that motivates viewers to take some kind of action.

Enhanced Brand Awareness The use of video advertisements can assist in the development of enhanced brand awareness and recognition. They make it possible for you to tell the story of your brand in a way that is more compelling.

Making Video Commercials That Work Effectively

The production of video advertisements that are successful calls for a methodical approach. The following are some suggestions for producing effective video advertisements:

Because people have such short attention spans, it is essential that your video advertisements be succinct and get straight to the point. Aim for a duration of no more than thirty seconds.

Focus on Emotion: Video advertisements are fantastic tools for communicating feeling. When you want to create an emotional connection with your audience, visuals, music, and storytelling are all powerful tools.

Show, Don't Tell Video is a visual medium; therefore, rather than simply telling your audience about your product or service, show them how it works through demonstration.

Include a Call to Action: Each and every video advertisement ought to comprise an accompanying call to action. Inspire the people who are viewing your content to take the next logical step, such as going to your website or making a purchase.

Optimize for Mobile Viewing It is important to optimize your advertisements for mobile viewing as a large number of people watch video advertisements on their mobile devices. When the sound is turned off, your audience should still be able to understand your message if you include subtitles or captions.

The Benefits of Including Video Ads in Your Retargeting Campaign

The use of video advertisements within a retargeting campaign is an excellent way to engage an audience and generate desired results. The following are some suggestions that can help you incorporate video advertisements into your retargeting campaign:

Your Audience Should Be Segmented: Your audience should be segmented based on their actions and the things that they are interested in. This will enable you to create video advertisements that are specific to the requirements and interests of the target audience.

Utilize Personalization: In order to produce video advertisements that are highly relevant to your target audience, utilize personalization. Retargeting allows you to display video advertisements to your audience that feature products that they have previously viewed or added to their shopping cart.

Select the Appropriate Platforms It is important that you select the appropriate platforms for your video advertisements. YouTube, Facebook, and Instagram are all fantastic platforms for video advertisements; however, each one possesses a unique set of advantages and disadvantages.

Measure Your Results You can determine how effective your video advertisements are by using metrics such as the number of views, the amount of engagement, and the conversion rate. Make use of this information to improve your targeting as well as the messaging you send.

To summarize, video advertisements are an effective method for retargeting campaigns to use. You can engage your target audience and drive results for your business by creating powerful video advertisements, integrating them into your retargeting campaign, and measuring the effectiveness of the ads' impact on your audience.

Chapter 8: Social Media Retargeting: Winning Sales with Facebook and Instagram Ads

The practice of retargeting users on social media is an effective strategy for increasing sales and conversions. Facebook and Instagram are two of the most popular social media platforms for retargeting campaigns, and both of these platforms offer a variety of tools and features that can assist you in reaching the audience you are trying to reach. In this chapter, we will talk about the advantages of retargeting on social media platforms and how to effectively create advertisements on Facebook and Instagram.

The Advantages of Retargeting with Social Media

Utilizing social media retargeting for your marketing campaigns comes with a number of advantages to take advantage of. Just a few of them are as follows:

You Can Reach a Larger Audience: Because Facebook and Instagram each have billions of users, you are able to reach a larger audience with these two platforms than you would with others.

Accurate Targeting Both Facebook and Instagram provide users with a variety of options for targeting, such as demographic targeting, interest targeting, and behavioral targeting. Because of this, you will be able to communicate effectively with the target audience.

Image ads, video ads, carousel ads, and a variety of other types of advertisements are just some of the ad types that can be purchased on Facebook and Instagram. This gives you the ability to select the format of the advertisement that caters to your message and audience in the most effective manner.

Developing Ads That Perform Well On Facebook And Instagram

A deliberate strategy is required to create advertisements that are successful on Facebook and Instagram. Here are some suggestions for writing advertisements that are compelling:

Pick the Right Ad Format To get the most out of your message and your audience, pick the ad format that works best for you. For instance, if you want to showcase a number of different products, you might select an ad format known as a carousel.

Utilize Eye-Catching Visuals Make use of high-quality visuals that are both captivating to the audience and effective in communicating your point. Your advertisement will be more noticeable if it makes use of eye-catching elements such as high-quality images, bold typography, and vibrant colors.

Maintain Clarity and Brevity in Your Communications: Be sure to maintain clarity and brevity in your communications. To encourage clicks and conversions, use headlines that are succinct and attention-grabbing, as well as calls to action.

Utilize Personalization and Dynamic Creative: In order to create advertisements that are highly relevant to your target audience, you should utilize personalization and dynamic creative. Retargeting allows you to display advertisements to your audience that feature products that they have previously viewed on your website or added to their shopping cart.

Incorporate a Call to Action: Each and every advertisement needs to incorporate a call to action. Inspire the people who are viewing your content to take the next logical step, such as going to your website or making a purchase.

Ads on Facebook and Instagram should be integrated into your retargeting campaign.

Ads on Facebook and Instagram can be an excellent way to engage your audience and drive results when they are incorporated into a retargeting campaign. The following are some suggestions for incorporating advertisements on Facebook and Instagram into your retargeting effort:

Make Use Of Facebook's Custom Audiences Feature To Create Custom Audiences You can make use of Facebook's Custom Audiences feature to create custom audiences based on the behavior and interests of individuals. This will enable you to create advertisements that are specific to the requirements and interests of the target audience.

Utilize Lookalike Audiences: The Lookalike Audiences feature on Facebook allows you to connect with new people who share characteristics with your current customers. This can help you reach a larger audience and identify new clients who might be interested in working with you.

Select the Appropriate Placement It is important that you select the appropriate location for your advertisements. Desktop, mobile, and the right-hand column are just some of the different placement options that are available on Facebook and Instagram. You should decide on the placement that serves both your message and your audience the best.

Keep an Eye on Your Results: When evaluating the efficacy of your advertisements, some useful metrics to look at include click-through rates, conversion rates, and return on ad spend. Make use of this information to improve your targeting as well as the messaging you send.

In conclusion, retargeting on social media is an effective strategy that can drive sales and conversions when used properly. You can engage your target audience and drive results for your business if you create ads that are effective, integrate them into your retargeting campaign, and monitor the results of these efforts. Facebook and Instagram are two examples of such platforms.

Chapter 9: Google Ads Retargeting: Reaching Customers on the Google Display Network

---

Retargeting with Google Ads is an effective method for reaching customers who are already familiar with your brand and have engaged with it in the past. You can persuade people who have previously interacted with your brand or visited your website to make a purchase from your business by displaying advertisements on the Google Display Network in such a way that they see those advertisements. In this chapter, we will discuss the advantages of using retargeting with Google Ads as well as the best practices for developing ads for use on the Google Display Network.

Advantages of Utilizing Retargeting with Google Ads

Utilizing Google Ads retargeting for your marketing campaigns comes with a number of advantages that should be considered. Just a few of them are as follows:

Reaching a Larger Audience: Because the Google Display Network is used by billions of people, it allows advertisers to reach a larger audience than they would be able to with other platforms.

Targeting Options: Google Ads gives users the ability to select from a variety of targeting options, such as demographic targeting, interest targeting, and behavioral targeting. Because of this, you will be able to communicate effectively with the target audience.

Formats for Advertisements: The Google Display Network makes available a variety of advertising formats, such as image advertisements, video advertisements, and many more. This gives you the ability to select the advertisement format that caters to both your message and your audience in the most effective manner.

Developing Ads That Are Compelling for the Google Display Network

A strategic approach is required in order to create advertisements on the Google Display Network that are successful. The following are some suggestions for writing advertisements that are persuasive:

Utilize Eye-Catching Visuals Make use of high-quality visuals that are both captivating to the audience and effective in communicating your point. Your advertisement will be more noticeable if it makes use of eye-catching elements such as high-quality images, bold typography, and vibrant colors.

Maintain Clarity and Brevity in Your Communications: Be sure to maintain clarity and brevity in your communications. To encourage clicks and conversions, use headlines that are succinct and attention-grabbing, as well as calls to action.

Utilize Personalization and Dynamic Creative: To produce advertisements that are highly relevant to your target audience, you should utilize personalization and dynamic creative. Retargeting allows you to display advertisements to your audience that feature products that they have previously viewed on your website or added to their shopping cart.

Incorporate a Call to Action: Each and every advertisement needs to incorporate a call to action. In order to get viewers to take the next step, which could be visiting your website or making a purchase, you should encourage them to do so.

The Retargeting Campaign You Run Should Include Google Ads Retargeting

Engaging your audience and driving results can be accomplished easily and effectively through the use of Google Ads retargeting, which should be incorporated into your retargeting campaign. The following are some suggestions for incorporating retargeting through Google Ads into your existing campaign:

Make Use Of Google's Custom Audiences Feature To Create Custom Audiences Make use of Google's Custom Audiences feature to create custom audiences based on the behavior and interests of individuals. This will enable you to create advertisements that are specific to the requirements and interests of the target audience.

Utilize RLSA (Remarketing Lists for Search Ads): Utilize RLSA to show ads to people who have previously visited your website when they search for related keywords on Google. In this way, you can generate repeat traffic to your website. This can help to improve the performance of your ads as well as increase the relevance of your advertisements.

Select the Appropriate Placement It is important that you select the appropriate location for your advertisements. Desktop, mobile, and in-app advertising are just some of the ad formats that can be utilized through the Google Display Network. You should decide on the placement that serves both your message and your audience the best.

Keep an Eye on Your Results. When evaluating the efficacy of your advertisements, some useful metrics to look at include click-through rates, conversion rates, and return on ad spend. Make use of this information to improve your targeting as well as the messaging you send.

In conclusion, Google Ads retargeting is an effective strategy for reaching out to customers who are already familiar with your brand and have engaged with it in the past. You can engage your target audience and drive results for your business by developing compelling advertisements to run on the Google Display Network, incorporating those advertisements into your retargeting campaign, and monitoring the outcomes of these efforts.

Chapter 10: Email Retargeting: Creating Personalized Email Campaigns that Convert

———

Customers who have already engaged with your brand can be effectively reached through email retargeting, which is a powerful marketing strategy. You can encourage people who have previously interacted with your brand or visited your website to make a purchase from your e-commerce platform by sending them relevant and personalized emails after they have interacted with your brand or visited your website. In this chapter, we will discuss the advantages of email retargeting as well as the steps necessary to develop successful email marketing campaigns that result in conversions.

The Advantages of Retargeting with Email

Using email retargeting as part of your retargeting campaigns can bring you a number of different benefits. Just a few of them are as follows:

Email has a higher open and click-through rate than many other forms of digital marketing, which is one reason why it is an efficient way to communicate with the people you want to reach.

Personalization: Since email gives you the ability to tailor your message to the recipient's actions and interests, you can make it more pertinent to the recipient's life and more interesting to read.

Email marketing is one of the most cost-effective forms of marketing, which makes it a fantastic choice for companies of any size and in any industry.

Developing Efficient Email Marketing Campaigns

Email marketing campaigns that are successful require a method that is well thought out. The following are some suggestions for developing email marketing campaigns that are successful:

Make Your Message More Relevant to the Recipient by Personalizing It Make your message more relevant to the recipient by personalizing it. This may involve addressing the customer by name, referring to products that the customer has viewed or added to their shopping cart, and personalizing your message to the customer based on their interests and the actions that they take.

Maintaining Clarity and Brevity in Your Message: Be sure to maintain clarity and brevity in your message. To encourage clicks and conversions, use headlines that are succinct and attention-grabbing, as well as calls to action.

Your Audience Should Be Segmented: Your audience should be segmented based on their actions and the things that they are interested in. Because of this, you will be able to design email campaigns that are specific to the requirements and interests of the target audience.

Make Use of Eye-Catching Visuals: To get people's attention and get your message across, use eye-catching visuals of a high quality, such as pictures and videos.

Include a Call to Action: Every email you send out should have a call to action included in it. Encourage recipients to take the next step, such as visiting your website or making a purchase, by providing them with a call to action.

Including Email Retargeting in Your Marketing Campaign to Target Customers

Engaging your audience and driving results can be achieved to a great extent by including email retargeting as part of your overall retargeting campaign. In order to successfully integrate email retargeting into your retargeting campaign, consider the following advice:

Utilize Automation: Make use of automation in order to activate email marketing campaigns based on the actions of the recipient. Someone who has added items to their shopping cart but has not yet completed their purchase, for instance, is eligible to receive an email titled "cart abandonment."

Personalize Your Emails You can create email campaigns that are highly relevant to your target audience by using personalization in the creation process. This may involve addressing the customer by name, referring to products that the customer has viewed or added to their shopping cart, and personalizing your message to the customer based on their interests and the actions that they take.

Test and Optimize: Run multiple tests with distinct iterations of your email marketing campaigns to determine which one has the most successful messaging and design. Measure the efficiency of each variant by referring to metrics such as open rates, click-through rates, and conversion rates.

Keep an Eye on Your Results: Monitoring the efficacy of your email marketing campaigns can be done through the use of metrics such as open rates, click-through rates, and conversion rates. Make use of this information to improve your targeting as well as the messaging you send.

In conclusion, email retargeting is an effective strategy that can be used to reach customers who have already engaged with your brand in the past. You can engage your target audience and drive results for your business by creating efficient email marketing campaigns, integrating those campaigns into your retargeting marketing campaign, and monitoring the results of those campaigns.

Chapter 11: Retargeting for E-commerce: Strategies for Increasing Sales and Customer Loyalty

In the world of online retail, retargeting is an effective strategy for boosting sales and maintaining customer loyalty. You can encourage people who have interacted with your brand in the past to make a purchase from your website by showing them advertisements and sending them personalized emails after they have done so. In this chapter, we are going to talk about the advantages of retargeting for e-commerce, as well as strategies for increasing sales and maintaining customer loyalty.

Retargeting has many advantages for online retailers.

Utilizing retargeting for online retailing brings with it a number of advantageous side effects. Just a few of them are as follows:

Increased Sales Retargeting customers with advertisements for products that they have already shown interest in or added to their shopping cart is one way to help increase sales.

Increased Customer Loyalty Retargeting can help to increase customer loyalty by demonstrating to customers that you appreciate the business they provide and are dedicated to making their shopping experience enjoyable.

Retargeting is one of the most cost-effective forms of marketing, which is why it is such a fantastic choice for e-commerce businesses of all sizes.

Methods for Increasing Sales and Maintaining the Loyalty of Customers

The following are some strategies that can be used to increase sales and customer loyalty in e-commerce through the use of retargeting:

Make Your Message More Relevant to the Recipient by Personalizing It Make your message more relevant to the recipient by personalizing it. This may involve addressing the customer by name, referring to products that the customer has viewed or added to their shopping cart, and personalizing your message to the customer based on their interests and the actions that they take.

Instill a Sense of Urgency: You can motivate customers to make a purchase by instilling a sense of urgency in them. For instance, you could highlight the fact that a product is moving quickly or provide a discount that is only available for a limited time.

Provide Incentives: Provide customers with various types of incentives in order to encourage them to make a purchase. Free shipping, a price reduction, or a free gift with purchase are some examples of this type of offer.

Utilize Dynamic Retargeting: Utilize dynamic retargeting to display advertisements to customers that feature products that they have viewed previously or added to their shopping cart. This can help to jog their memory about products that they were considering purchasing and encourage them to go ahead and make the acquisition.

Develop a Customer Loyalty Program Develop a customer loyalty program to recognize and thank customers for their continued business. This may involve providing benefits such as special discounts, free shipping, and other advantages.

Implementing Retargeting Into Your Online Shopping Strategy

It is a fantastic method for boosting sales and maintaining customer loyalty if your e-commerce strategy includes retargeting as an element.

The following are some suggestions that can help you incorporate retargeting into your overall e-commerce strategy:

Customers who have interacted with your brand can be reached via a variety of different channels, such as Facebook, Instagram, and email, so make use of as many of these as possible. Your retargeting campaign might benefit from this, and end up being more successful as a result.

Monitor Your Metrics You can monitor the efficiency of your retargeting campaign by using metrics such as click-through rates, conversion rates, and return on ad spend. Make use of this information to improve your targeting as well as the messaging you send.

Test and Improve: To determine which version of your retargeting campaign has the most successful messaging and design, you should conduct tests using a variety of different iterations. When evaluating the efficacy of each variant, it is helpful to make use of metrics such as click-through rates, conversion rates, and return on ad spend.

Make Use Of Frequency Capping You Can Limit The Number Of Times A Customer Sees Your Ad By Making Use Of Frequency Capping. This can be helpful in preventing ad fatigue and ensuring that the appropriate individuals see your message at the appropriate time.

In e-commerce, retargeting is an effective strategy for increasing sales and maintaining customer loyalty, as the previous paragraph argued. You can encourage customers to make a purchase and keep coming back for more by using personalization, creating a sense of urgency, offering incentives, using dynamic retargeting, and creating a loyalty program. These are all ways that customers can be incentivized to make a purchase. You can generate results for your company and build a customer base that is loyal to you by including retargeting in the strategy you use for your online store and monitoring the metrics it produces.

Chapter 12: Retargeting for B2B: Reaching Decision Makers with Account-Based Marketing

---

When it comes to B2B marketing, retargeting is a powerful strategy that can be used to reach decision makers. You can show ads and send personalized emails to decision makers at the companies you are targeting if you use account-based marketing. In this chapter, we will talk about the advantages of using retargeting for B2B marketing as well as strategies for using account-based marketing to get in front of decision makers.

The Value of Retargeting for Business to Business

When it comes to marketing to other businesses, retargeting offers a number of advantages. Just a few of them are as follows:

Retargeting enables you to create targeted messaging for decision makers at the companies that you are targeting, which can then be sent to those decision makers.

Increased Brand Awareness If you use retargeting, you can help increase the brand awareness of decision makers, which in turn increases the likelihood that they will consider your company for future business.

Retargeting is one of the most cost-effective forms of marketing, which makes it a fantastic choice for businesses that cater to other businesses, regardless of their size.

Account-based marketing tactics that can be used to more effectively engage decision-makers

The following are some strategies that can be used to reach decision makers in B2B settings through the use of retargeting and account-based marketing:

Identify Key Decision Makers One of the first things you should do is determine who the key decision makers are at the companies you are going after. This could include C-level executives, department heads, and other decision makers who are involved in the process of purchasing the product or service.

Make Your Message More Relevant to the Recipient by Personalizing It Make your message more relevant to the recipient by personalizing it. This may involve mentioning the company's name, the industry in which it operates, or particular pain points that your solution can alleviate.

Establish a Convincing Value Proposition It is essential that you establish a convincing value proposition in order to effectively communicate the benefits of your solution to the decision makers that you are focusing on.

Employ a Number of Different Channels To communicate with the decision makers at the companies that you are interested in, you should make use of a number of different channels, such as LinkedIn, email, and display ads. Your account-based marketing campaign might benefit from this, as it could help make it more effective.

Retargeting as an Element of Your Business-to-Business Marketing Strategy

Retargeting is an excellent method for reaching decision makers and driving results for your company, and it should be an integral part of your B2B marketing strategy. Here are some tips for integrating retargeting into your B2B marketing strategy:

Utilize a Number of Different Touchpoints To communicate with decision makers at the businesses that you are interested in, utilize a number of different touchpoints, such as email, display ads, and LinkedIn. Your account-based marketing campaign may benefit from this, which can help to make it more effective.

Monitor Your Metrics You can monitor the efficiency of your retargeting campaign by using metrics such as click-through rates, conversion rates, and return on ad spend. Make use of this information to improve your targeting as well as the messaging you send.

Test and Optimize: To determine which version of your retargeting campaign has the most successful messaging and design, you should conduct tests using a variety of different variants. When evaluating the efficacy of each variant, it is helpful to make use of metrics such as click-through rates, conversion rates, and return on ad spend.

Target Decision Makers Who Have Interacted With Your Company in the Past Retargeting lists can be used to target decision makers who have previously interacted with your company. Your return on investment (ROI) and the effectiveness of your retargeting campaign may both improve as a result of this.

In conclusion, retargeting is an effective strategy that can be used in B2B marketing to communicate with decision makers. You can create targeted messaging that resonates with decision makers at the companies you are targeting by utilizing account-based marketing, personalization, and a compelling value proposition. You can drive results for your company and build long-lasting relationships with decision makers in your target market if you incorporate retargeting into your B2B marketing strategy and monitor your metrics.

Chapter 13: Retargeting for Local Businesses: Winning Customers in Your Community

The practice of retargeting is an effective strategy for local businesses that are interested in acquiring new customers in their community. You can encourage customers who have interacted with your company in the past to come back and make a purchase by sending them advertisements and personalizing the emails you send to them. In this chapter, we will discuss the benefits of retargeting for local businesses as well as strategies for winning customers in your community. Specifically, we will be focusing on the local market.

Retargeting's Benefits to Local Companies and Organizations

Utilizing retargeting is beneficial for local businesses in a number of different ways. Just a few of them are as follows:

Retargeting can help to increase foot traffic to your business by reminding people who have previously visited your site about the products and services you offer.

Increased Customer Loyalty Retargeting can help to increase customer loyalty by demonstrating to customers that you appreciate the business they provide and are dedicated to making their shopping experience enjoyable.

Retargeting is one of the most cost-effective forms of marketing, which makes it a fantastic choice for regional companies of all sizes.

Methods for Attracting and Keeping Customers in Your Local Community

The following are some strategies you can use to win customers in your community by utilizing retargeting:

Make Your Message More Relevant to the Recipient by Personalizing It Make your message more relevant to the recipient by personalizing it. This can be accomplished by referring to the customer's previous purchases, customizing your message to the customer's interests and behaviors, and emphasizing your connection to the local community.

Develop a Sense of Urgency: In order to motivate customers to make a purchase, you should create a sense of urgency. For instance, you could highlight the fact that a product is moving quickly or provide a discount that is only available for a limited time.

Provide Incentives: Provide customers with various types of incentives in order to encourage them to make a purchase. This might come in the form of a price reduction or a free present with the purchase.

Utilize Location-Based Targeting: Show advertisements to people who are located in your local community by utilizing location-based targeting. This can assist in making your message more relevant to its audience and encourage people to pay a visit to your place of business.

Retargeting as a Component of Your Local Business Strategy

It is a great way to win customers and build loyalty in your community to have your local business incorporate retargeting as part of its overall strategy. The following are some suggestions for incorporating retargeting into the strategy of your local business:

Utilize a Number of Different Channels To communicate with customers who have already interacted with your company, you should make use of a number of different channels, such as email, Facebook, and Instagram. Your retargeting campaign might benefit from this, and end up being more successful as a result.

Monitor Your Metrics You can monitor the efficiency of your retargeting campaign by using metrics such as click-through rates, conversion rates, and return on ad spend. Make use of this information to improve your targeting as well as the messaging you send.

Test and Improve: To determine which version of your retargeting campaign has the most successful messaging and design, you should conduct tests using a variety of different iterations. When evaluating the efficacy of each variant, it is helpful to make use of metrics such as click-through rates, conversion rates, and return on ad spend.

Utilize Retargeting Lists: Retargeting lists allow you to focus your marketing efforts on individuals who have previously interacted with your company. Your return on investment (ROI) and the effectiveness of your retargeting campaign may both improve as a result of this.

In conclusion, retargeting is an effective strategy for local businesses that are interested in acquiring new customers in their community. You are able to create targeted messaging that will resonate with your local audience if you use personalization, urgency, incentives, and location-based targeting in your communications with them. You will be able to drive results for your company and build long-lasting relationships with customers in your community if you incorporate retargeting into the strategy you use for your local business and monitor the metrics associated with it.

Chapter 14: Retargeting for Events: Promoting Your Event with Targeted Ads

---

Retargeting is a powerful method that can be used to promote events and increase attendance at those events. You can encourage people to register for and attend your event by sending them advertisements and personalizing the emails you send to them after they have expressed interest in it. In this chapter, we will discuss the advantages of using retargeting for events as well as strategies for promoting your event through the use of targeted advertisements.

Retargeting's Advantages When It Comes to Events

Utilizing retargeting as a strategy for events comes with a number of advantageous side effects. Just a few of them are as follows:

Attendance Can Be Boosted Through Retargeting: One way that retargeting can help boost attendance is by reminding people who have already expressed interest in your event and encouraging them to register for it.

Increased Return on Investment (ROI) Retargeting is one of the most cost-effective methods of marketing, which makes it a fantastic choice for events of any size. Retargeting can help to improve the return on investment (ROI) of your event by increasing the number of attendees.

Retargeting gives you the ability to create targeted messaging for individuals who have previously expressed an interest in your event, which increases the likelihood that those individuals will sign up for the event and attend.

Methods for Effectively Marketing Your Occasion through the Use of Specific Ads

The following are some strategies that can be used to promote your event with targeted advertisements using retargeting:

Determine Who You Want to Attend Your Event Determine who you want to attend your event, taking into account things like their demographics, interests, and behaviors. Having this information will make it easier for you to craft targeted messaging that will resonate with them.

Make Your Message More Relevant to the Recipient by Personalizing It Make your message more relevant to the recipient by personalizing it. This may include making a reference to the individual's prior attendance at one of your events, pointing out sessions that are pertinent to the individual's interests, or adapting your message to their specific position or the industry in which they work.

Develop a Sense of Urgency: Make people feel as though they need to act quickly in order to sign up for your event. For instance, you could highlight the fact that tickets are going quickly or provide a discount for a limited amount of time.

Utilize Retargeting Lists You can target individuals who have previously demonstrated an interest in your event by utilizing retargeting lists. People who have visited the website for your event or registered for one of your previous events could fall into this category.

Retargeting as a Component of Your Event Promotion Strategy

It is a great way to increase attendance at your event and improve the return on investment of your event to include retargeting as part of your event promotion strategy. The following are some suggestions for incorporating retargeting into the overall strategy of promoting your event:

Utilize a Number of Different Channels If you want to reach people who have expressed interest in your event, you should make use of a number of different channels, such as Facebook, LinkedIn, and email. Your retargeting campaign might benefit from this, and end up being more successful as a result.

Monitor Your Metrics You can monitor the efficiency of your retargeting campaign by using metrics such as click-through rates, conversion rates, and return on ad spend. Make use of this information to improve your targeting as well as the messaging you send.

Test and Optimize: To determine which version of your retargeting campaign has the most successful messaging and design, you should conduct tests using a variety of different variants. When evaluating the efficacy of each variant, it is helpful to make use of metrics such as click-through rates, conversion rates, and return on ad spend.

Utilize Frequency Capping You can limit the amount of times a person will see your advertisement by utilizing frequency capping. This can be helpful in preventing ad fatigue and ensuring that the appropriate individuals see your message at the appropriate time.

In conclusion, retargeting is an effective strategy that can be used to promote events and increase attendance at those events. You can create targeted messaging that resonates with your target audience and encourages them to register for and attend your event by employing personalization, urgency, retargeting lists, and multiple channels in your communication with them. You can drive results for your event and build a loyal following of attendees by including retargeting as part of your event promotion strategy and monitoring your metrics.

Chapter 15: Retargeting for Mobile: Reaching Customers on the Go

Retargeting is an effective method for reaching customers while they are on the move by delivering targeted advertisements to their mobile devices. People who have interacted with your company on their mobile devices can be encouraged to take action and make a purchase by displaying advertisements to them and sending them messages that are personalized to them. In this chapter, we will talk about the advantages of using retargeting for mobile, as well as different strategies for communicating with customers who are on the move.

Advantages to Retargeting on Mobile Devices

Utilizing retargeting on mobile devices comes with a number of distinct advantages. Just a few of them are as follows:

Increased Number of Conversions: Retargeting can help increase the number of conversions your business sees by reminding people who have interacted with your company on mobile about the products and services you offer.

Retargeting can help to improve the user experience by displaying relevant ads and personalized messages to customers while they are on the go. This can help to improve the user experience on mobile devices.

Because it is one of the most cost-effective methods of marketing, retargeting is an excellent choice for companies of any size and in any industry.

Ways to Communicate with Customers Who Are Always on the Move

Using retargeting to communicate with customers while they are on the move can be done in a few different ways, including the following:

Make Your Message More Relevant to the Recipient by Personalizing It Make your message more relevant to the recipient by personalizing it. This may include making a reference to the customer's previous purchases, adapting your message to the customer's interests and behaviors, and emphasizing your connection to the local community.

Develop a Sense of Urgency: In order to motivate customers to take action, you should create a sense of urgency. For instance, you could highlight the fact that a product is moving quickly or provide a discount that is only available for a limited time.

Utilize Location-Based Targeting You can show advertisements to people who are in your local area by utilizing location-based targeting. This can assist in making your message more relevant to its intended audience and encourage people to take action.

Employ a Mobile-Friendly Design Make sure that your advertisements and messages are simple to read and navigate on mobile devices by employing a design that is mobile-friendly. This may include the utilization of larger fonts, distinct calls-to-action, and landing pages that are optimized for mobile devices.

Retargeting as a Component of Your Mobile Marketing Strategy

If you want to reach customers while they are on the go and drive results for your company, integrating retargeting into your mobile marketing strategy is a great way to do so. Here are some tips for integrating retargeting into your mobile marketing strategy:

Utilize a Number of Different Channels To communicate with clients who have interacted with your company via mobile, you should utilize a number of different channels, such as Facebook, Instagram, and email.

Your retargeting campaign might benefit from this, and end up being more successful as a result.

Monitor Your Metrics You can monitor the efficiency of your retargeting campaign by using metrics such as click-through rates, conversion rates, and return on ad spend. Make use of this information to improve your targeting as well as the messaging you send.

Test and Optimize: To determine which version of your retargeting campaign has the most successful messaging and design, you should conduct tests using a variety of different variants. When evaluating the efficacy of each variant, it is helpful to make use of metrics such as click-through rates, conversion rates, and return on ad spend.

Make Use Of Retargeting Lists: Make use of retargeting lists in order to target people who have previously interacted with your company on their mobile devices. Your return on investment (ROI) and the effectiveness of your retargeting campaign may both improve as a result of this.

In conclusion, retargeting is an effective method for reaching customers while they are on the move through the use of targeted advertisements and personalized messages delivered on mobile devices. You can create targeted messaging that resonates with your mobile audience and encourages them to take action by making use of personalization, urgency, location-based targeting, and design that is mobile-friendly. You can generate results for your company and build long-lasting relationships with customers by including retargeting in your mobile marketing strategy and monitoring your metrics. This will allow you to conduct business while on the move.

Chapter 16: Retargeting and Customer Lifetime Value: Increasing Revenue with Repeat Customers

R etargeting is a powerful technique for increasing revenue with repeat customers by encouraging them to make additional purchases. This is accomplished by displaying targeted advertisements on third-party websites. You can increase the lifetime value of customers by displaying advertisements to them and sending them personalized emails after they have already made a purchase. This will encourage them to come back to your store and make additional purchases. In this chapter, we are going to talk about the advantages of retargeting in order to increase customer lifetime value, as well as strategies for increasing revenue with repeat customers.

The Value of Retargeting Customers Based on Their Long-Term Investment

Utilizing retargeting as part of a strategy to increase customer lifetime value can result in a number of positive outcomes. Just a few of them are as follows:

Increased Revenue: One of the ways that retargeting can help to increase revenue is by encouraging existing customers to make additional purchases, which in turn increases the customers' lifetime value.

Increased Customer Loyalty Retargeting can help to increase customer loyalty by demonstrating to customers that you appreciate the business they provide and are dedicated to making their shopping experience enjoyable.

Because it is one of the most cost-effective methods of marketing, retargeting is an excellent choice for companies of any size and in any industry.

Methods for Increasing Profits from Current Clients Who Buy Again and Again

The following are some strategies that can be used to increase revenue through repeat customers by using retargeting:

Make Your Message More Relevant to the Recipient by Personalizing It Make your message more relevant to the recipient by personalizing it. This could include referring to the customer's previous purchases, making product suggestions based on the customer's interests and behaviors, and highlighting exclusive offers that are only available to loyal customers.

Provide Incentives: Provide incentives in order to encourage customers to make repeat purchases. This could take the form of a price reduction or a free present along with the purchase for repeat customers.

Make Use Of Retargeting Lists You can target customers who have already purchased from your company in the past by making use of retargeting lists. Your return on investment (ROI) and the effectiveness of your retargeting campaign may both improve as a result of this.

Utilize Upselling and Cross-Selling: In order to encourage customers to make additional purchases, it is important to utilize upselling and cross-selling. This could involve making recommendations for complementary products or providing an option for a more luxurious version of a product that the customer has already purchased.

Implementing Retargeting as Part of Your Strategy to Increase Customer Lifetime Value

Retargeting should be incorporated into your strategy for maximizing the lifetime value of customers as it is an excellent way to both boost revenue and strengthen loyalty among your existing customer base. Here are some suggestions for incorporating retargeting into your strategy for increasing customer lifetime value:

Customers who have already made a purchase can be reached through a variety of mediums, including email, social media, and display advertisements, if you make use of multiple channels. Your retargeting campaign might benefit from this, and end up being more successful as a result.

Monitor Your Metrics You can monitor the efficiency of your retargeting campaign by using metrics such as click-through rates, conversion rates, and return on ad spend. Make use of this information to improve your targeting as well as the messaging you send.

Test and Optimize: To determine which version of your retargeting campaign has the most successful messaging and design, you should conduct tests using a variety of different variants. When evaluating the efficacy of each variant, it is helpful to make use of metrics such as click-through rates, conversion rates, and return on ad spend.

Utilize Segmentation: Make use of segmentation in order to target particular groups of customers based on the purchasing patterns and actions they have taken in the past. This can be useful in the process of creating targeted messaging that speaks to each group in a way that resonates with them and encourages them to make additional purchases.

In conclusion, retargeting is an effective strategy for increasing revenue with repeat customers and building up the lifetime value of customers. You can create targeted messaging that resonates with your existing customers and encourages them to make additional purchases by using techniques such as personalization, incentives, upselling and cross-selling, and retargeting lists. You can also use retargeting lists. You can generate results for your company and build long-lasting relationships with your customers if you include retargeting in the strategy you use to calculate the lifetime value of your customers and monitor the metrics associated with that strategy.

Chapter 17: Retargeting Metrics: Analyzing Campaign Performance and Optimizing for Success

In order to ensure that retargeting campaigns are operating at their full potential, they need to undergo ongoing analysis and optimization. In this chapter, we will go over the significance of retargeting metrics, how to measure the success of a campaign, and various strategies for optimizing retargeting efforts.

Retargeting metrics is important, so keep that in mind.

Metrics for retargeting are essential because they offer insightful information about how well your retargeting campaigns are doing. You will be able to evaluate the success of your campaigns and determine where there is room for improvement if you keep track of these metrics. The following are some important metrics regarding retargeting:

Click-Through Rate (CTR) is a metric that measures the ratio of the number of clicks your advertisements receive to the total number of times they are displayed. A high CTR shows that your ads are interesting to the people you are trying to reach and are therefore relevant to them.

Conversion Rate: The conversion rate is calculated by dividing the total number of clicks received by an advertisement by the number of people who actually complete the desired action (such as making a purchase or filling out a form). A high conversion rate indicates that your advertisements are successfully provoking action from the people who are intended to receive them.

Return on Ad Spend (ROAS) is a metric that calculates the amount of revenue generated by your advertisements in comparison to the amount of money spent on advertisements. If your ROAS is high, it means that the retargeting campaign you are running is successful in terms of generating a positive return on investment.

Assessing the Results of a Campaign

It is important to set specific goals for your retargeting campaign and track metrics over time in order to measure how successful the campaign has been. The following are some steps that can be taken to measure the success of a campaign:

Define Goals: Before beginning your retargeting campaign, it is important to define clear goals for the campaign, such as increasing the number of conversions or improving the return on investment.

Pick Your Metrics Pick metrics that are pertinent to your goals, such as click-through rate (CTR), conversion rate (ROAS), and return on ad spend (ROAS).

Establish Benchmarks: Establish benchmarks for your metrics by basing them on industry standards or on the performance of previous campaigns.

Metrics Should Be Tracked: Metrics should be tracked over time to measure the success of a campaign and to identify areas that could use improvement.

Improving the Performance of Retargeting Campaigns

It is essential to perform consistent analysis and make necessary adjustments to your strategy in order to get the most out of your retargeting campaigns. The following is a list of strategies that can help you optimize your retargeting campaigns:

Utilize A/B Testing: Utilize A/B testing to compare various versions of your advertisements or messaging in order to determine which strategy is the most successful.

Targeting Should Be Refined: To increase relevance and engagement, you should fine-tune your targeting based on the actions, interests, and demographics of your customers.

Improve your return on investment by optimizing your bids by adjusting your bid strategy based on metrics such as click-through rate and conversion rate.

Refresh the Creative: It is important to frequently refresh your creative in order to maintain an engaging and modern design and messaging.

Adjust the Frequency: If you want to avoid ad fatigue and make sure that your message is received by the appropriate audience at the appropriate time, you should adjust the frequency of your advertisements.

Think About Cross-Device Retargeting Cross-device retargeting is something you should think about if you want to reach customers on multiple devices and boost engagement.

Retargeting Metrics Should Be Included in Your Marketing Strategy

The incorporation of retargeting metrics into your marketing strategy is an essential step that must be taken in order to maximize the effectiveness of your retargeting campaigns and generate results for your company. Incorporating retargeting metrics into your marketing strategy can be accomplished with the help of the following tips:

Utilize Analytical Tools Tracking retargeting metrics and monitoring campaign performance can be accomplished with the assistance of analytical tools such as Google Analytics and Facebook Pixel.

Regularly Monitor Metrics It is important to regularly monitor your retargeting metrics in order to identify areas that could be improved and to optimize your campaign strategy.

To Demonstrate the Effectiveness of Your Retargeting Strategy, Share the Results with Stakeholders: To demonstrate the efficacy of your retargeting strategy, share the results of your retargeting metrics and the performance of your campaign with stakeholders, such as executives or customers.

Utilize Metrics to Guide Strategy Utilize retargeting metrics as a way to guide your campaign strategy and make adjustments to your approach based on how well it is performing.

Chapter 18: Advanced Retargeting Tactics: Cross-Device Retargeting and Lookalike Audiences

Retargeting campaigns are an effective method for communicating with customers who have already demonstrated an interest in your company. These campaigns allow you to connect with customers who have shown interest in your company. On the other hand, there are more sophisticated methods of retargeting that can bring your campaigns to the next level. Cross-device retargeting and lookalike audience targeting are going to be the topics that we cover in this chapter regarding advanced retargeting strategies.

Retargeting Across Multiple Devices

Cross-device retargeting is a strategy that allows you to target customers across multiple devices, such as desktop computers, tablets, and smartphones. It is also known as "cross-device remarketing." Targeting customers across all of their devices can increase the amount of time they spend engaged with a brand's content and the number of times they make a purchase. This strategy is important because consumers use multiple devices throughout the purchasing process.

The following are some strategies for retargeting across multiple devices:

Utilize Multi-Device Tracking To track the behavior of customers across all of their devices, you should make use of a multi-device tracking tool. Some examples of such tools include Google's cross-device reports and Facebook's cross-device attribution tool.

Ensure That Your Messaging And Creative Are Consistent Across All Devices In order to provide your customers with a seamless experience, it is important that you ensure that your messaging and creative are consistent across all devices.

Employ Dynamic Creative: Employ dynamic creative to display personalized advertisements that are tailored to the device and behavior of each individual customer.

Make Bid Adjustments for Each Device Make bid adjustments for each device to optimize your advertising spend and maximize your return on investment (ROI).

Lookalike Audiences

Lookalike audiences are a powerful targeting tool that enables you to reach new customers who are similar to your existing customers. Lookalike audiences allow you to expand your customer base. You can create a lookalike audience by analyzing the data you already have on your customers. This audience will have characteristics in common with the original customers, such as interests, behaviors, and demographics.

Here are some strategies for using lookalike audiences:

Conduct an Analysis of Customer Data Conduct an analysis of your existing customer data in order to identify patterns and traits that are shared by your most valuable customers.

Construct a Seed Audience: Construct a seed audience by basing it on your most valuable customers or segments with the highest conversion rates.

Using a lookalike audience tool, such as Facebook Lookalike Audiences or Google Similar Audiences, you can create a new audience that has characteristics that are similar to those of your seed audience. This new audience is referred to as a "lookalike audience."

Experiment with a number of different permutations of your lookalike audience in order to zero in on the strategy that yields the best results. Measure the effectiveness of each variation by referring to metrics such as click-through rate and conversion rate.

Adapting Your Retargeting Strategy to Include Cross-Device Retargeting and Lookalike Audiences

If you want to increase the amount of engagement and conversions you get from your target audience, integrating cross-device retargeting and lookalike audiences into your retargeting strategy can help. The following are some suggestions that can help you incorporate these strategies into your retargeting strategy:

Utilize Multi-Channel Retargeting: Utilize a multi-channel retargeting strategy that incorporates cross-device retargeting and lookalike audiences in order to communicate with customers across a number of different devices and platforms.

Keep an Eye on Your Metrics Be sure to keep an eye on your retargeting metrics, such as click-through rate (CTR) and conversion rate, in order to determine how successful your cross-device retargeting and lookalike audience campaigns are.

Make Adjustments to Your Strategy Based on Its Performance Make adjustments to your strategy based on how well your cross-device retargeting and lookalike audience campaigns have been performing. To improve your targeting and messaging, make use of metrics like click-through-rate (CTR) and conversion rate.

Conduct experiments and make adjustments: In order to determine which strategy is the most successful, conduct experiments using different iterations of your cross-device retargeting and lookalike audience campaigns. Measure the effectiveness of each variation by referring to metrics such as click-through rate and conversion rate.

Chapter 19: Retargeting Compliance: Staying Within Legal and Ethical Guidelines

R etargeting campaigns are a powerful tool for reaching out to customers who have already demonstrated an interest in your company and engaging with them further. Nevertheless, it is essential to make certain that your campaigns are in accordance with all applicable legal and ethical guidelines. In this chapter, we will go over the significance of retargeting compliance, the legal requirements that must be met by retargeting campaigns, and the strategies that can be implemented to ensure compliance with ethical guidelines.

A Focus on Retargeting Compliance and Its Importance

Compliance with retargeting guidelines is essential because doing so helps to preserve the trustworthiness of your brand and safeguards the personal information of your customers. Retargeting campaigns that do not comply with the regulations can cause reputational harm to your brand and result in legal penalties. Building trust with your clientele and preserving the efficiency of your retargeting campaigns are both possible outcomes that result from adhering to the relevant legal and ethical standards.

Legal Requirements for Retargeting Campaigns

Businesses are required to comply with a number of legal requirements in order to run successful retargeting campaigns. The following are some important prerequisites:

Retargeting campaigns are required to comply with data protection regulations, such as the General Data Protection Regulation (GDPR) in the European Union and the California Consumer Privacy Act (CCPA) in the United States. Before a company can collect and use the personal data of its customers, these regulations require that the company first obtain the customers' consent.

Standards for Advertising Retargeting campaigns are required to comply with advertising standards, such as the guidelines established by the Federal Trade Commission (FTC) in the United States. Because of these guidelines, companies are required to reveal any sponsored content and to check that their advertisements are honest and do not mislead customers.

Retargeting campaigns have to be in accordance with age restrictions, such as the Children's Online Privacy Protection Act (COPPA) in the United States. Before collecting information from children younger than 13, businesses are required by these regulations to first obtain the consent of the children's parents.

Methods for Maintaining Compliance with the Ethical Standards

When developing and executing retargeting campaigns, it is essential to act in accordance with both the legal requirements and the ethical guidelines that have been established. Listed below are some approaches that can be utilized to maintain compliance with ethical standards:

Be Transparent: Maintain an honest and open dialogue with your existing clientele regarding your retargeting efforts. It should be made perfectly clear that you are employing retargeting ads, and you should also provide information about the collection and utilization of customer data.

Customers who do not wish to be shown retargeting advertisements should have the option to opt out, and this option should be made available to them. It is important to respect the preferences of customers and provide them with clear instructions on how to opt out of retargeting campaigns.

Customers should not be followed around with retargeting ads; this is known as "stalking." You should limit the frequency of your advertisements and stay away from showing people ads for goods or services they have already bought.

Keep Your Ads Relevant: Make sure that your retargeting ads still have some relevance. Avoid showing ads that are generic or unrelated to the customer's behavior and instead show ads that are relevant to the customer's interests.

Adjust as Necessary: Make sure that you are regularly monitoring your retargeting campaigns to ensure that they are adhering to all of the relevant ethical and legal standards. Make any necessary adjustments to your strategy in order to remain compliant with these standards.

Complying with regulations regarding retargeting as part of your marketing strategy

The incorporation of retargeting compliance into your marketing strategy is an essential step that must be taken in order to earn the trust of your clientele and safeguard the reputation of your brand. The following are some suggestions that can help you integrate compliance with retargeting into your marketing strategy:

Self-Education: It is important that you educate yourself on the legal and ethical guidelines that apply to retargeting campaigns in your region. Maintain current knowledge of any alterations that may be made to these guidelines.

Prepare Your Group to Face: Provide your marketing team with training on the legal and ethical standards that should be followed for retargeting campaigns. Make sure that they are aware of the significance of compliance and the steps to follow in order to remain in accordance with these guidelines.

Make Sure Your Tools Are in Compliance Always make sure your tools are in compliance with the laws and ethical standards in place. Utilize retargeting tools such as those that provide opt-out choices and are compliant with data protection regulations, for instance.

Maintain Constant Vigilance Over Your Campaigns You should maintain constant vigilance over your retargeting campaigns to maintain compliance with legal and ethical standards. Measure the efficiency and success of your campaigns with the help of tools like analytics and the comments and suggestions of your target audience.

Make Changes to Your Strategy Make any necessary changes to your retargeting strategy in order to ensure compliance with all applicable legal and ethical regulations. Optimize your campaigns with the help of data and feedback while ensuring that you remain compliant.

In conclusion, ensuring that your retargeting campaigns are compliant is an essential concern for any business that employs this marketing strategy. Businesses have the opportunity to strengthen their relationships with their clientele and maintain the efficiency of their marketing efforts when they adhere to legal and ethical guidelines. It is essential to educate yourself as well as your team, make use of tools that are compliant, monitor your campaigns, and adjust your strategy as necessary in order to remain in compliance with the guidelines. With these strategies in place, businesses will be able to use retargeting campaigns to reach and engage with the audience they are trying to reach while still adhering to the appropriate ethical and legal standards.

Chapter 20: The Future of Retargeting: Emerging Trends and Technologies to Watch

R etargeting campaigns have evolved into an indispensable component of the marketing strategies employed by many companies. The advancement of technology has resulted in the emergence of a number of new trends and technologies that will have a significant impact on the future of retargeting. In this chapter, we will talk about some of the new trends and technologies that will be important to keep an eye on in the future of retargeting.

AI and ML (machine learning and artificial intelligence)

Emerging technologies such as artificial intelligence (AI) and machine learning (ML) are currently being incorporated into a wide variety of marketing strategies, one of which is retargeting. The analysis of customer data and behavior, the customization of retargeting ads, and the optimization of marketing campaigns for maximum efficiency are all possible with the help of these technologies for businesses.

For instance, artificial intelligence can be used to forecast which customers are most likely to become paying clients based on the demographics and behaviors of those customers. This information can be put to use to create personalized retargeting advertisements that are specific to the preferences and actions of each individual customer. In addition, machine learning algorithms can be used to optimize advertising campaigns in real time by adjusting bids and targeting in order to achieve the greatest number of conversions.

Voice Search as well as Intelligent Speakers

Voice searches and smart speakers, such as the Amazon Echo and the Google Home, are gaining a lot of popularity these days. Because more and more people are turning to voice search to locate goods and services, companies will need to modify their retargeting campaigns in order to reach users who use voice search.

Developing ad copy that is compatible with voice search and keywords that are optimized for voice search queries is one approach to achieving this goal. Users of smart speakers can also be targeted with retargeting ads that are specific to their location, interests, and behavior by targeting them with ads that are relevant to those factors.

Augmented Reality

Augmented reality (AR) is a relatively new technology that is already being implemented by some companies to improve the overall experience they provide for their customers. Customers will be able to more easily visualize products in their own environment before making a purchase if interactive retargeting ads are created using augmented reality (AR) technology.

For instance, a store that sells furniture could use augmented reality (AR) to develop a retargeting advertisement that gives customers the opportunity to visualize how a sofa would appear in their own living room before purchasing it. By giving customers a more immersive shopping experience, this type of interactive advertisement can increase the level of engagement as well as the number of sales made.

Personalization

Personalization in marketing has been on the rise for some time, but its significance in retargeting campaigns is only growing. Customers have come to expect individualized and customized experiences that are catered to their preferences and actions, and companies that are unable to meet these expectations risk losing business to competitors who can.

Retargeting campaigns allow for personalization to be accomplished by utilizing customer data and behavior to generate targeted advertisements that are pertinent to the interests of each individual customer. The customer's location, browsing history, and purchasing behavior can all be taken into consideration when designing ads with dynamic creative. These ads can then be displayed to the customer.

Retargeting Across Multiple Devices

Cross-device retargeting is already being utilized by a large number of businesses, and it is anticipated that it will play an even more significant role in the future of retargeting. Businesses that are able to target their customers across all of their devices will have an advantage over those that are unable to do so because customers are increasingly using multiple devices to browse and shop online.

Cross-device retargeting is something that can be accomplished through the utilization of tools like Google's cross-device reports or Facebook's cross-device attribution tool, both of which are designed to track the behavior of customers across multiple devices. Customers can then be presented with personalized advertisements based on their past actions and the preferences they have expressed, regardless of the device they are using.

In conclusion, the future of retargeting looks promising, as there are many new trends and technologies on the horizon that will shape the way in which businesses communicate with and interact with their respective target audiences. In the coming years, it will be important to keep an eye on a number of trends and technologies, including artificial intelligence and machine learning, voice search and smart speakers, augmented reality, personalization, and cross-device retargeting, to name just a few. Businesses that are able to adjust to these trends and incorporate them into their retargeting campaigns will be in a better position to achieve success in the highly competitive online market.

Also by B. Vincent

Affiliate Marketing
Affiliate Marketing
Affiliate Marketing

Standalone
Business Employee Discipline
Affiliate Recruiting
Business Layoffs & Firings
Business and Entrepreneur Guide
Business Remote Workforce
Career Transition
Project Management
Precision Targeting
Professional Development
Strategic Planning
Content Marketing
Imminent List Building
Getting Past GateKeepers
Banner Ads
Bookkeeping
Bridge Pages
Business Acquisition

Business Bogging
Business Communication Course
Marketing Automation
Better Meetings
Business Conflict Resolution
Business Culture Course
Conversion Optimization
Creative Solutions
Employee Recruitment
Startup Capital
Employee Incentives
Employee Mentoring
Followership
Servant Leadership
Human Resources
Team Building
Freelancing
Funnel Building
Geo Targeting
Goal Setting
Immanent List Building
Lead Generation
Leadership Course
Leadership Transition
Leadership vs Management
LinkedIn Ads
LinkedIn Marketing
Messenger Marketing
New Management
Newsfeed Ads
Search Ads
Online Learning
Sales Webinars

Side Hustles
Split Testing
Twitter Timeline Advertising
Earning Additional Income Through Side Hustles: Begin Earning Money Immediately
Making a Living Through Blogging: Earn Money Working From Home
Create Bonuses for Affiliate Marketing: Your Success Is Encompassed by Your Bonuses
Internet Marketing Success: The Most Effective Traffic-Driving Strategies
JV Recruiting: Joint Ventures Partnerships and Affiliates
Secrets to List Building
Step-by-Step Facebook Marketing: Discover How To Create A Strategy That Will Help You Grow Your Business
Banner Advertising: Traffic Can Be Boosted by Banner Ads
Affiliate Marketing
Improve Your Marketing Strategy with Internet Marketing
Outsourcing Helps You Save Time and Money
Choosing the Right Content and Marketing for Social Media
Make Products That Will Sell
Launching a Product for Affiliate Marketing
Pinterest as a Marketing Tool
Retargeting Mastery: Winning Sales with Online Strategies

About the Publisher

Accepting manuscripts in the most categories. We love to help people get their words available to the world.

Revival Waves of Glory focus is to provide more options to be published. We do traditional paperbacks, hardcovers, audio books and ebooks all over the world. A traditional royalty-based publisher that offers self-publishing options, Revival Waves provides a very author friendly and transparent publishing process, with President Bill Vincent involved in the full process of your book. Send us your manuscript and we will contact you as soon as possible.

Contact: Bill Vincent at rwgpublishing@yahoo.com

www.ingramcontent.com/pod-product-compliance
Lightning Source LLC
Chambersburg PA
CBHW031246050326
40690CB00007B/968